AF253429

# THE RESILIENCE OF A WOMAN

*Stories of Faith, Love, and Perseverance*

SHAWNTA JACKSON

Shawnta Jackson

*The Resilience of a Woman*

ISBN: 978-0-578-33121-8

Printed in the United States of America

# DEDICATION

This book is dedicated to my only child, Zachary. I have always liked his name because when I was growing up, all of the cool kids were named Zach. Also, while I was pregnant, I received confirmation for his name and his life when I read Zechariah 1:1-6 in the Bible.

I know that I make you proud and that you love me because you tell me so often. I am proud to be your mother and will love you eternally. Always remember that God assigned angels to watch over me and that I gave some of my angels to you.

# CONTENTS

# PREFACE

**In my first book,** *The Journal of a Woman with Lived Experiences,* I shared twenty-one of my real-life personal journal entries that served as moments of reflection, clarity, venting, affirmation, prayer, planning, and gratitude for me. I felt that my experiences and thoughts would be beneficial to help people to organize their thoughts about themselves and their relationships, their choices, and how they process their emotions.

I encouraged readers to fully participate in the process by responding to my journal prompts based on the same themes of my personal entries. I received positive reviews from both men and women as well as testimonials about how my journal entries inspired them to exercise these forms of self-reflection, self-care, and self-therapy.

Considering that we all grow and change, I owe it to myself and my readers to follow up and be honest about where I am at now in life and if any of my thoughts or status on the various topics and themes I wrote about in my first book, *The Journal of a Woman with Lived Experiences,* have changed. Honestly, I am still processing many of these subjects and while we do grow and things change, life is still a process. I am still me. My experiences are still my experiences.

Am I wiser? Yes. Am I more in tune with myself and God? Yes. Have I grown? Yes. Have some things remained the same? Probably so, maybe and yes. This is why I am sharing this sequel to my first book. The only difference is that you are my journal, I am writing directly to you unless otherwise noted. It is all from my heart and spirit.

# CHAPTER 1

## Owning My Story:
## The Power of Storytelling

*Forgiveness, Understanding, Acceptance, and Reality*

**The first journal entry** in *The Journal of a Woman with Lived Experiences* shed light on the unhealthy relationship I had with my ex-husband, my son's father. I ended the entry by saying that there is still an opportunity for them to build a stronger relationship together, and if not, so be it.

I still feel the same way. I have to accept things for what they are and accept people for who they are and proceed accordingly. Even so, I wanted to take the time to share what it is that I actually have to say to my son about his dad. The first thing that comes to mind is when my son was about six years old. I told him that his dad loves him but does not know how to show it. My son replied, "I know."

After thirteen missed birthdays, zero games, missed milestones, consecutive years with no visits and inconsistent communication, I now tell my son not to have any expectations about his dad and just to accept him for who he is. I also tell him that people can change, but only time will tell if this will happen. I know men who did not have a relationship with their dads during adolescence but later in adulthood they were able to build a bond and create a friendship.

While my son has not seen or spoken to his paternal grandmother since he was two years old, every now and then I remind him of her name. She has never called, but follows him on social media, which he barely uses. I will never forget when my son was about nine years old and we went on a road trip with my mother to Atlanta where his paternal grandmother lived. I called her thinking that she would want to see him. Although she was home, she used work as an excuse not to see him even after I offered to meet her in the parking lot at her job. After that call ended, I vowed that she would never have to worry about me reaching out to her again to see my son, and I have not and will not unless he asks me to. If or when she wants to meet, she can contact my son, who will respond as he sees fit. I am confident that I raised my son to have good judgment.

My son does have five older siblings (four sisters and one brother) from his dad. He is in contact with all his siblings or at least they know how to reach him. During our visits to Chicago, I made sure that he visited his three sisters that live there. Also, during a trip to Atlanta, I took him to meet his fourth sister for the first time. Their dad has never brought them together as a family, at least not with my son. No holidays, birthdays, or summers. In my opinion, this has negatively impacted them all as children and as young adults. They need their father to be a leader and good role model. However, I do understand that sometimes absence is better if relationships are going to be unhealthy and toxic. This is the sad truth, but it is reality.

Even though my son barely knows his dad's family members, I am happy that he knows who his siblings are and that they have somewhat of a connection. Also, my son is an uncle and hopefully will be able to spend time with all of his nieces and nephews someday. He has spent years growing a relationship with one of them because I am the godmother to his oldest niece.

I was once their bonus mother, and I loved them and cared for them as if they were my own children. It is not their fault that things between their dad and I did not work out, and it should not be an issue for them to communicate with their little brother, my son, which in the past seemed to be the case. However, the issue was really about communicating with me because of their fear of how their dad might react. Either way, I have a loving and healthy relationship with my son. As long as they mean well, his siblings and dad are welcome to be a part of his life if they choose to do so. I just will not be the one to play matchmaker or to occupy my head space because I have done my part and they are all old enough to make choices and decisions for themselves.

As for my relationship with my son's dad, it is unfortunately almost nonexistent. We will speak every blue moon, but it is hard for me to trust and respect him because of our history and his inconsistencies as a parent. I feel like he left me no choice but to be a single-parent mother. I have always made 100 percent of the parenting decisions and bore 100 percent of the responsibility for my son's security and overall well-being. The fact is that I have not been able to depend on his father to help me provide for or support or nurture our son, who is now growing into young adulthood. Parents should be able to consistently and effectively communicate when it comes to the welfare of their child, but since I cannot turn back the clock, all I can do is move forward. Like the advice that I give to my son, I simply accept his dad for who he is, and I accept the situation for what it is. My son is old enough to communicate with his dad without me and when or if his dad is ready to change, God will guide him. My role is to support my son.

My focus is making sure my son is loved, healthy, mentally strong, and properly prepared to function in this world and serve as a productive member of society. Even though it is sad that his dad has not been active in his life, I do believe that everything has worked out for the best. As I mentioned in my first book, *The Journal of a Woman with Lived Experiences*, my son did not grow up witnessing domestic abuse nor has he experienced dysfunction or trauma. He has never witnessed a man disrespecting me. I feel that my son is fortunate and protected.

My son is also fortunate in that he experiences love from my father and uncles, who model a positive manhood, wisdom, self-discipline, and understanding, especially from my father, who is equivalent to an angel sent by God to guide and protect us. Also, there are other men in my life who have been genuine and nice to my son. I am appreciative of their sincerity, thoughtfulness, and positive role modeling.

# Your Thoughts
*Owning My Story: The Power of Storytelling*
*Forgiveness, Understanding, Acceptance, and Reality*

What are your key takeaways from this chapter? What story or stories in your life are worthy of consideration for forgiveness, understanding, acceptance, and reality? Are you there yet or are you still processing your thoughts and feelings? Be honest with yourself.

# CHAPTER 2

## The Benefits of Positive Affirmations and Gratitude

**I got this.** I can do this. God is with me. All the resources that I need are provided for me. I am successful, I attract success, and I am surrounded by the right people. My relationships are healthy and fulfilling. Everything that I need is supplied to me in abundance because I never want for anything. My life is peaceful. I am a happy and confident person. My body knows what is best for me and heals itself. I am healthy and radiate and attract positivity. I ask for and receive God's guidance. I give and receive love.

Positive affirmations are also known as affirmative prayer, scientific prayer, and spiritual mind treatment. As much as prayer is spiritual, it is also mental. Either way, I believe that the answer to our prayers should be in our prayers. As written in the Bible in Matthew 7:7, "Ask, and it shall be given you; seek, and ye shall find; knock, and it shall be opened unto you." Another popular example of an affirmative prayer is the prayer of King David in Psalm 23. "The Lord is my and I shall not want...."

It is also written in Surah (Chapter) 13:11 of the Quran: "Indeed, Allah will not change the condition of a people until they change what is in themselves." While Buddhists do not believe in any kind of deity or god, the spiritual tradition of Buddhism focuses on personal enlightenment and in the words of the Buddha, "With our thoughts we make the world."

There are a lot of things going on in this world, and there are massive amounts of subliminal and explicit messages such as advertisements and news commentary that we are exposed to. These messages can affect both our subconscious (unconscious) mind and conscious mind. In my opinion, just like the constant exposure to messages from outside influences ultimately impacts our thoughts, mood, beliefs, decision-making, and behavior – constant internal messages to ourselves impacts us as well.

I have days and sometimes consecutive days or weeks when I am not motivated to do anything, I am not happy, or I am just simply lost during these times. I have realized that this only happens when I stop being consistent with my positive affirmations, meditation, prayers, and journaling. Because I have learned this about myself, I personally feel like I have no choice but to continue these practices to stay in my "zone."

When I am in my zone, I am able to take advantage of the opportunities surrounding me and maintain positive relationships. I am able to manage my time better, which allows me to maintain a healthier lifestyle because this now creates a space in which I am motivated to make smoothies and exercise on a regular basis, which as we all know has its own mental, physiological, and physical benefits.

Luckily for us, we have free will. We all have the ability to choose to program or reprogram our minds. Why not choose the positive and enlightened path not only to motivate ourselves but to manifest our thoughts into reality through the practice of positive affirmations, demonstrations of faith, and the implementation of the next best steps? Try to be flexible and adapt to new ways and break free from a cycle of old thinking patterns.

In addition to positive affirmations, I have also created a habit of acknowledging what I am grateful for. As soon as I wake up but am barely able to open my eyes, I acknowledge what I am grateful for as a form of reflection and as a prayer to God. Other times I write words of gratitude in my journal or simply recite my feelings out loud. I also try to consistently journal before bedtime to reflect on what I am grateful for as well as my experiences, accomplishments, and lessons learned for the day.

As I mentioned in my previous book, I believe that gratitude also produces spiritual benefits such as continued blessings from God. Additionally, there are scientifically proven benefits of gratitude. Gratitude improves physical health, psychological health, and self-esteem. It also enhances empathy, reduces aggression, and increases mental strength.[1]

Before I end this chapter, I want you to open your heart and think about five things that you are grateful for no matter how big or small they may seem. Writing them down and placing the paper somewhere where you will see it often will also serve as a reminder for you to continue the practice. The same is true for positive affirmations, which you can write down or simply recite to yourself. There are many online audio recordings and videos that can guide you – my favorites are from Bob Baker, an author, speaker, and video creator who produces morning affirmations, guided meditations, and inspirational talks. Below are examples of my favorite affirmations that you can recite to yourself but before you do, focus your mind and take a few deep breaths. Repeat these affirmations to yourself on a regular basis.

1    Morin, Amy. "7 Scientifically Proven Benefits of Gratitude." *Psychology Today*. April 3, 2015. Accessed October 23, 2021. https://www.psychologytoday.com/us/blog/what-mentally-strong-people-dont-do/201504/7-scientifically-proven-benefits-gratitude.

**Affirmations:**

*I am fully present.*

*I am grateful for another day.*

*I am accepting of myself and others.*

*I deserve happiness.*

*I have the strength and confidence to handle whatever comes my way.*

*My body knows what to do to heal itself.*

*I honor my body by trusting the signals it sends to me.*

*Money comes to me in expected and unexpected ways.*

*I give and accept love.*

*I am enough.*

*I am worthy.*

*I am becoming the best version of myself.*

*I am manifesting my dreams into reality.*

# Your Thoughts
## *The Benefits of Positive Affirmations and Gratitude*

What are your key takeaways from this chapter? Write positive affirmations to yourself and about yourself as well as five things that you are grateful for.

__________________________________________________

__________________________________________________

__________________________________________________

__________________________________________________

__________________________________________________

__________________________________________________

__________________________________________________

__________________________________________________

__________________________________________________

__________________________________________________

__________________________________________________

__________________________________________________

__________________________________________________

__________________________________________________

__________________________________________________

__________________________________________________

# CHAPTER 3

## Love and Relationships

**A common theme in** my journal entries has been love and relationships: *Manifesting Love; Expecting Love; Allowing Yourself to Trust Someone Else; Balancing Independence and Relationships; Unconditional Love and Commitment;* and *Shallow Thinking.* I even shared that falling in love on a boat in the Mediterranean was on my bucket list, and as silly as it may seem to some people, it is still there.

One of my key takeaways in my first book was my belief that love is intentional (deliberate and conscious) and can be manifested. Meaning that we have to make ourselves available to give and receive love. I also shared that I was not sure if I really believed in or expected to find love and true companionship. I will use this chapter to share my current thoughts about love, which required me to really dig deep within me to be honest with myself and you.

So, how do I feel about love? I definitely want love and am capable of loving myself, another person and everything that we love together. I know exactly what love is and now I think it is more about making yourself available and not passing on the opportunity to love and be loved. Love and being in a relationship are choices. You can choose to love someone. You can choose to commit to someone and build a life with that person. We just have to choose the right reasons and the right person at the right time. This is the hard part because how do we know what is right?

As good as our fairy tales and stories that we tell ourselves about our dream relationship and partner are, we have to learn to get past our emotions and to think sensibly. This is where our self-assessment and values come into play. Do you even know enough about yourself to maintain and grow a healthy relationship with someone? How do you know that you are compatible with someone? I think the answer is to take your time and for you both to discuss your ideal life and scenarios. What are "deal breakers" for the both of you? There are card games, online guides, and books that will help to guide your conversations, which is a great way to bond regardless of your relationship status with that person.

In addition to "deal breakers" I also think it is important to use an asset-based approach, which is focusing on the strengths and positive attributes about that person and not focusing so much on what you do not like. You should know enough about yourself and feel comfortable expressing your physical, intellectual, emotional, mental, social, spiritual, and financial beliefs as well as your needs, such as your likes and desires. You should also be open and willing to learn about your partner's beliefs, needs, likes, and desires to help both of you to determine if you should continue seeing each other. If you are already in a relationship, these discussions will help you to determine how you both can move forward by improving the relationship and supporting each other.

Along with love being a choice, I believe love happens in phases and that relationships happen in phases as well. I also think that love is evolving because people develop and change. This means that we should expect for the person that we fall in love with on day one to have changing needs. We should expect our needs and desires to change as well and be willing to be open about communicating those changes. This is a healthy development as long as we can change for the better. To love is also to understand and respect each other's feelings.

I had a conversation with a guy whom I told that I believe in unconditional love. He told me that loving your children is unconditional love because no matter what, they belong to you and that cannot be changed. He said that romantic love cannot be unconditional. This is because everyone has expectations that contradict the notion of not having strings attached or loving someone no matter what the circumstance or without limits. I guess he is right because if people really loved unconditionally, the divorce rate would not be so high.

Also, I think we all need to come to the realization that love is not enough. For those of us who are not jaded and still believe in love, we should include it as a criterion for commitment and life partnership but understand that love does not hold much weight on its own. Keep in mind that love is an emotion, and anyone making life decisions based on only emotions lacks discernment, wisdom, and understanding.

For me, the foundation for a loving and respectful relationship includes having a reciprocal amount of trust, communication, and respect. However, before that foundation is laid, no man will get anywhere with me unless there is attraction and chemistry. His physical appearance tells me a lot about his lifestyle and values, which may or may not be in alignment with mine. A man's physical appearance helps me to determine our compatibility on a surface level. For example, I value good health and hygiene. Without a man telling me anything about his lifestyle, his body shape, eyes, teeth, and nails tell me everything that I initially need to know in order to move forward with him or not.

With all that said, the real question that you probably want to know is why am I 40 years old, intelligent, fine, but single? I must be crazy, right? Or better yet, I must be one of those I-N-D-E-P-E-N-D-E-N-T women who does not need a man, right? Nope. None of the above. It is just not my time.

God willing, I have at least fifty-nine more years on this earth, and like all of the women in my family, I am aging gracefully. I am consistently elevating myself, and many of the guys that I have met are not capable or emotionally available to join me on my life's journey. No matter how much they want to or how much I want them to, I cannot force what is not there even when I have tried. I actually believe in love and happiness and because I am not desperate to be in a relationship, I am willing to be patient and wait for the right person to enter my life if he has not already.

Nevertheless, one thing I am going to stop doing is being so nice to these men and allowing them the privilege of having access to see me at their convenience. Also, I need to stop taking advantage of them and stop using them for and at my convenience.

In closing, below is an excerpt from my personal journal entry written after the release of my first book.

*Dear love, you have always been around. You have always been with me. You molded me and taught me lessons. You were there to comfort me when my love was not accepted and betrayed. You are with me now and are standing by waiting for the right moment to reveal yourself to me like you have never done before.*

*You understand me. You are very understanding. You are going to continuously improve my life. I am ready for you. Please reveal yourself to me or better yet, open my heart so that I may reveal myself to you.*

# Your Thoughts
*Love and Relationships*

What are your key takeaways from this chapter? What are your thoughts about love and relationships? Whether you are in a relationship or not, write down the pros and cons of a person being in a relationship with you. Also, what are your "deal breakers" and why? Is there anything about yourself or your standards that you should work on changing? Be honest with yourself.

# CHAPTER 4

## Letters to My Boyfriends

**On public platforms and** through written communications with my readers I often joke about having multiple boyfriends and at times I post public messages to my "boyfriends," who are usually men that I do not know in everyday life who openly engage with and support my endeavors. The following message is dedicated to them.

### *Dear Boyfriends,*

*First, I want to start off by saying that you are appreciated, and the world needs you. We need you. I need you. The world cannot exist without you. However, we want you to do more than exist. We want you to reach your highest potential, live your life's purpose, and achieve the highest level of success in all areas of your life.*

*Regardless of where you are in life at this moment, it is never too late to become a better version of yourself. It is never too late to start doing the work of self-reflection and self-improvement. It is never too late to decide on who you must become in order to be your best self. It is never too late to start doing the work to heal from any negative situation in your past or present. It is never too late to learn. It is never too late to love and be loved.*

*In addition to the message above, I also would like to share real life journal entries that I have written since the release of my first book to men who I actually date or have dated in some capacity and that, like you, will be reading these entries for the first time. I am a little embarrassed* and nervous to share, but I addressed dating, love, and relationships so heavily in my previous published journal entries that it is only right for me to be transparent with my readers about my current dating life (at the time of writing this book), which has improved since my last book even though I am still single, learning lessons about love, and experiencing slight disappointments.

### *Dear Boyfriend,*

Today when I reached out to you, I was not expecting you to answer let alone call me back. I also was not expecting to speak to you for so long. I honestly thought I had lost your attention. I appreciate the fact that I was able to share my feelings and thoughts with you.

I do not expect anything from you. I do not even expect anything from myself but to stay humble and depend on God to guide me. When it comes to dating, my heart, and relationships, I do not seem to have the best judgment. I am starting to feel like it is normal for love to hurt. It is like having a broken heart is a prerequisite for finding true love.

No, that statement is not directed toward you. It is just how I feel at the moment.

I am glad that you are healthy and well. I am glad that you are recovering. Maybe one day you will let me take care of you for a few days. I know that you are independent and can take care of yourself, but I am a giver and nurturer by nature. I would not mind spoiling you. I would just be treating you the way I want to be treated.

I wonder if God is going to give me true love any time soon. I know it is possible and I know it will happen. I just wonder when and with whom. It would be surreal, and I probably would not believe that it was really happening to me.

Because of my past experiences and what I consider to be flaws, I convinced myself that I was unlovable. As much as I want it to happen and I know it is possible, I am not so sure that it will really happen. It is hard for me to imagine someone that I am heartfelt about feeling the same way about me and that feeling being strong enough to bring me into his world and him into mine.


**Dear Boyfriend,**

I cannot sleep. I wish I could, but I cannot. I wish my mind was clear, but it is not. The light is hurting my eyes, but I cannot stand to sit in the dark. I have no interest in scrolling through social media or reading online content. I am writing "just because." Because I need to clear my mind and figure out what is on my mind. I do not even have to figure it out; I just want to empty my thoughts enough so that I can hear God and receive comfort. To receive guidance and advice. I know not to lean on my own understanding. I just have to let go of trying to control everything. Actually, I lose control if things do not go my way.

*What is really bothering me is that I did not get a chance to speak to you today. I wanted to share my day with you. I can barely stop monitoring my phone and barely sleep because I anticipate your phone calls. I am comfortable and got used to talking to you. I am spoiled, I admit. I worry that you will change your mind about me or that I may come across as burdensome or needy.*

**Dear Boyfriend,**

*Back on the love thing. It is something that I really know nothing about and that I am unfamiliar with. I have sought it. I have asked for it. I have prayed for it, and I have waited for it. In the process, I wonder if it is too late for me? Did I pass up on opportunities or did I ruin it for myself by giving my time and self to the wrong men?*

*I have written in my journal so many times about a guy and how I like him and how he might be the one. I have also written a lot about how a particular guy is not the one and why. My heart and feelings get hurt, and I get disappointed or run away but yet, I have hope. I have faith that God will reveal my life partner to me. I ask for what is right by God's standards, not mine. I ask for someone to love me and for me to give my love freely and willingly in return.*

**Dear Boyfriend,**

*I really miss you. Today was a really productive day. This week and last week were particularly* good. I was intentional about changing my thought processes, managing my time, and staying focused. It is working.

I often think about lying next to you or going on a walk while I tell you about whatever is on my mind. I miss the random kisses that we gave to each other. I miss watching TV with you too. I really enjoyed our moments together. Everything was and is so memorable. I really appreciate our time together, and I appreciate you. I know that you appreciate me as well.

There is so much that I want to talk to you about. I want to learn more about you. I want to learn about what makes you upset and what motivates you. I want to learn you but based on your words, you seem to have built a wall that makes you emotionally unavailable or resistant to vulnerability. You seem to be jaded. The truth is that our intentions and level of openness are different.

While I too am cautious, I do want to build a foundation for what could be a long-term relationship. For me, there has to be intention. I want to date for a purpose. My goal is not to just be someone's "friend." I may be wrong or jumping to conclusions, but I am not a mind reader and regardless of my sentiments about you, I am a very rational person or at least I think I am.

We all make time for who and what we value. If we are not on the same page, I can understand and accept that. I also understand that I am sensitive to rejection and may pay too much attention to and expect and seek signs of rejection. Either way, I do not have it in me to occupy my time, feelings, and thoughts with someone who is not willing to do the same or display it. I value reciprocity.

# Your Thoughts
## *Letters to My Boyfriends*

What are your key takeaways from this chapter? What person in your past, present, or future would you write a letter to? If no one were there to judge you, what would you write?

_______________________________________________

_______________________________________________

_______________________________________________

_______________________________________________

_______________________________________________

_______________________________________________

_______________________________________________

_______________________________________________

_______________________________________________

_______________________________________________

_______________________________________________

_______________________________________________

_______________________________________________

_______________________________________________

_______________________________________________

_______________________________________________

# CHAPTER 5

# Self-Validation, Fear, and Sacrifice

**In my first book** I explained that the level of confidence in our own thoughts affects our self-validation, which is a continuous practice for me. Also, in addition to confidence, I think that self-validation has a lot to do with worrying about what other people think or seeking approval from others to feel assured, worthy, or successful. Our contributions, worth, abundance, and standards of beauty should not be determined by the opinions of others. Our parenting style, food choices, business plan, and life goals do not need to be vetted by people who are not responsible for our well-being and happiness. I am responsible for my happiness and fulfillment in life. You are responsible for your own happiness and fulfillment in life. Other people are there to support us, but they do not make or break us.

I admit that my feeling embarrassed or silly about doing certain things ultimately comes from worrying about how I may appear to others. In the past, my concern about the judgment or opinions of others slowed down my progress and outcomes in many areas of my personal and business life. That is why I practice positive affirmations, write notes to myself, listen to motivational speeches, and more. While it is not a huge issue for me, I have to continuously train my mind not to self-destruct based on the opinions of others or what I think might be the opinion of others.

Along with our thoughts, there may actually be people in our lives who express their opinions whether they are solicited or not. I think it is important to recognize these people for who they are and consider their intentions and the validity of their words before allowing yourself to absorb these external influences about what appears to be about you. However, based on my experiences, their opinions are really about themselves. People will push their personal desires, goals, and insecurities onto you if you allow them to, and this is not always intentional.

Some people are deliberate and know exactly what they are doing, and others are unaware of their actions. That is why I encourage you to consider people's intentions and use your judgment in how you will respond, react, and move forward with those persons. Nevertheless, you still need to pay attention to and acknowledge patterns in people's behaviors regardless of their intent because it is important to surround yourself with the right people who will support your growth and not hinder it.

Also, while I welcome and enjoy accolades, that is not my motivation or fuel for why I exist or pursue certain endeavors because that is not sincere. That means that I would be giving away my power to other people, and what happens if they decide to no longer acknowledge me or give me accolades? Do I stop being who I am called to be and doing what I am called to do? No, I do not think so. I know that I am not for everyone and that I will not be able to win the hearts of every person that I encounter or who encounters me. I accept that not everyone will like, understand, or appreciate me and my contributions and you should accept this fact as well.

I am Shawnta Jackson. I have a track record of integrity, commitment, servitude, sincerity, value, accomplishments, and uplifting other people. I am not pretending to be anyone else, and I am okay with making temporary sacrifices, letting go of people, and gaining new connections on my timeline and in my own authentic way. I know who I am and what I bring to the table, and I am not going to sell myself short or sell my soul for the approval or validation of others. I recognize healthy and unhealthy patterns within myself and because I am self-aware, I recognize when my shortcomings are becoming pitfalls and I know when it is time to correct them and become more committed to feeding my own thoughts and self-confidence.

As it relates to dating, as much as I like men and want to be in a committed relationship, I do not seek validation or approval from them either. Of course, I want to please my man and be appealing to him but not at the expense of losing myself or my own happiness and self-worth.

Finally, I do not compare myself to others. Instead, I learn from others and celebrate their accomplishments. I choose not to compare myself to others because I know that we all have different life experiences and paths. Often what is meant for someone else is not meant for me and vice versa. Furthermore, you never know what people are going through or what they have endured to achieve whatever it is that they set out to do. You also do not know the level of support or the resources they started with. For example, someone may have inherited a business or had the privilege of living in a family member's basement rent free while launching their business; and meanwhile you live as the head of a household and do not have the luxury of not paying your rent or mortgage while you launch your business. Is it fair to compare the two? No.

Focus on building yourself up through positive affirmations, prayer, and manifestation. Validate yourself by investing in yourself and surrounding yourself with positive people. Be who you are and always change for the betterment of yourself, not for others.

# *Your Thoughts*
## *Self-Validation, Fear, and Sacrifice*

What are your key takeaways from this chapter? What are your thoughts about self-validation, fear, and sacrifice?

# CHAPTER 6

# Perseverance, Resilience, and Faith

**As written in the** Bible in Hebrew 11:1, "Now faith is the substance of things hoped for, the evidence of things not seen." In Hinduism, faith in the self and its eternal existence is important. As defined in the Merriam-Webster dictionary, perseverance "is the continued effort to do or achieve something despite difficulties, failure, or opposition." Similar to perseverance, resilience is the ability to get through difficult times and essentially "bounce back." Resilient people are not easily defeated.

As I mentioned in the beginning of this book and in my previous book, there is power in storytelling. In addition to being heard and owning my own story, I want to share my testimonies throughout various stages of my life to help demonstrate my belief that if you practice faith and exhibit perseverance and resilience, you too will get through life's challenges wiser and stronger. This will benefit you and the people you care about in the long term.

My first significant display of faith and resilience was when the 24-year-old me made a spontaneous decision to leave her life behind in Chicago. As explained in *The Journal of a Woman with Lived Experiences*, I had three pairs of dirty clothes from a road trip, $200 in my possession, and my 11-month-old baby boy with me when I arrived in Las Vegas. I had the battered woman syndrome – emotional, behavioral, and psychological effects as a result of domestic abuse and did not know it, but I knew enough not to go back home to my husband in Chicago, even though I had left before and come back.

The first time I left him was when my husband made my nose bleed when I was pregnant, but I only went a few miles away and for a few days. The second time I left was after he snatched and pulled the phone cord out of the wall while I was on it with my girlfriend. He cornered me in the bathroom and told me that he would beat me until I was black and blue because he did not like a comment about him that he over-heard me saying. That day, I sat outside in the backyard for hours with my son until I was sure that he had left the house. I cannot remember if it was the same week or not, but I left for Las Vegas without telling him. I do not remember packing many belongings. I believe my mom bought my plane ticket and because my son was under the age of two, he flew for free. I did not have much money, but I found a storage facility near the airport with a space big enough for my car. The first month was free and I used my mom's address. I took a cab to the airport and stayed in Las Vegas with my mom for about a month before I returned to Chicago.

The third and fourth times that I left my husband was the story that I told in my first book which is now all a backstory to me explaining how I demonstrated faith and resilience. I literally walked away with nothing, and once I did acquire a few things, including money in the bank, my ex-husband made me go to the bank and withdraw what he thought was all of my money because in his mind anything that I had was because of him. Therefore, it belonged to him. My son was about two years old when this happened, and we were divorced for about six months.

Because of my ex-husband's erratic, controlling, and unpredictable behavior and because I did not have the energy, I never took him to court for child support and alimony enforcement, which still is true to this day. I decided that I was better off figuring things out on my own and utilizing my fam-ily's support when I needed it. I knew that I was going to be okay and that I would eventually "come out on top."

I had a Bachelor of Arts Degree in Public Relations, and tried to move from Las Vegas as soon as possible, but I could not find a wage that I could live on elsewhere. So, I decided to stay in Las Vegas, and I worked at my family's construction company until I became a full-time real estate agent and a loan officer. Although I was performing well in the real estate industry, I saw signs that the market was crashing and I decided to start a business, a concierge service in which I would provide business and marketing support to executives. That business never launched successfully, so I decided to work with my family part-time and I applied for and was accepted into graduate school at the University of Nevada, Las Vegas.

My intention the entire time was to leave Las Vegas and move to the East Coast with a lucrative job. However, I knew that the job market was very competitive and while I had the family support, I also knew that I needed to complete graduate school as quickly as possible and build as many relationships as I could because I knew that I could only live on my small budget and limited income for so long before I fell into a deep hole. In fact, the housing rental rates in Las Vegas in 2009 were so high that I could only afford to buy a condominium or townhome. Paying a mortgage was cheaper than paying rent. My dad gave me $3000 for my Federal Housing Administration (FHA) down payment and I bought a bank-owned property, a townhome for myself and my son.

After I purchased my townhome, I stopped working for my family and began to focus on my full-time graduate career. Luckily, my son was enrolled in a full-time kindergarten class, which eliminated the cost that I would have to pay for childcare. If a family member was not able to pick up my son after school or watch over him while I had classes, I would take my son to class with me or drop him off at the Boys & Girls

Club near campus that only charged about $20 for an annual membership. Sometimes, I would take him to the club, which closed around 6:30 p.m., and during my 15-minute break during class at 6:15 p.m. I would pick him up and bring him with me during the second half of my class.

As I mentioned, I knew that I could only sustain that lifestyle for so long. I was living off credit cards and received $15 per hour in part-time pay, but through my faith, resilience, and persistence, I made my way. I started graduate school in August 2009 and graduated in December 2010 with my Master of Public Health Degree. In addition to graduating with a 3.75 grade point average, during this short period of time I had two internships, one graduate assistantship, a part-time job in the field, and I served as a student member of the statewide public health association. I was offered a full-time salaried position with full benefits at the local health department two months after my graduation in February 2011. I started as a health educator at the Health Department in March 2011. All of that sacrifice, hard work, and persistence had paid off.

While working at the Health Department I excelled in everything that I did and after being there for nearly two-and-a-half years, I realized that there was no opportunity for growth and that I had enough faith in my experience and track record that I was now ready to move to the East Coast. However, how I was going to get there became the next unknown event and accomplishment considering that I really wanted to move to New York. However, I also traveled to Houston, Atlanta, and Washington D.C. looking for employment opportunities. I decided that New York was too expensive, and that Houston and Atlanta were not a great fit for me, so I pursued Washington D.C., which I had also visited with my dad when I was 16 years old. He took me to the steps of the U.S. Capitol Building and told me that I was going to work there some day. I was very defiant and told him that I would not work there. However, once I convinced my coworkers at the Health Department to use our conference travel funds to attend a health policy and advocacy summit in Washington D.C., I became open to the idea of working in the U.S. Capitol Building. This technically has not happened yet, but I have attended meetings and events there.

My Health Department coworkers and I attended the policy and advocacy summit meeting in March 2013. The keynote speaker at the conference was one of the best orators that I had seen in person in my lifetime. He talked about health equity in a way that I had never heard before, and in addition to me everyone in the room was amazed and inspired by his speech and presentation, so much so that they formed a line to greet and take a picture with him. Now keep in mind that my purpose for visiting D.C. was to network and identify job opportunities. With that said, I decided that I was going to be the last person to speak with him, and I stood next to him and managed the line by serving as his photography assistant before the event staff asked him to move to another room so that they could continue with the summit's schedule.

I was the last person to speak with this outstanding keynote speaker, who also was a professor and founding director of a center within a school of public health at a state university in nearby Maryland. It was a Sunday afternoon. I was not seeking a job from him, but I needed a mentor and wanted advice on the next best steps I should take in order to identify a job in the D.C. area. He told me to contact his administrative assistant to schedule an appointment and I told him that this plan was not going to work because I was leaving for Las

Vegas on that upcoming Tuesday. Monday was the only day that we could meet.

My persistence worked because I received a call from the speaker's administrative assistant on that early Monday morning asking me to meet him at his office in Maryland. Mind you, I was staying at a hotel in D.C. with no transportation. I rented a car and drove to the university. On my way there, I stopped at a copy shop to print and buy a three-ring binder with tabs to create a portfolio to share with him. I always documented my accomplishments and stored my files using an online cloud storage system in preparation for a day like this when I needed to highlight my talent.

When I walked into the conference room for what I thought was an informational interview, the director and a colleague were sitting at the conference table on speaker phone with another colleague. I immediately pulled out my notepad and actively participated in the meeting. I ended up spending about six hours with the director that day and before I left, I told him that I would like to work with him if an opportunity was available. He then proceeded to tell me that he could not promise me anything and before he could finish the sentence, I hugged him with excitement and told him, "Thank you," as if I already had a position. After returning to Las Vegas and many back-and-forth emails and to be honest, dwindling hope on my part, he reached out to me eight months later to ask me if I was still interested in a job.

I stepped out on faith and resigned from my job in Las Vegas, rented my townhome to a young married couple, and moved to Maryland in December 2013 with my nine-year-old son, who was in the middle of his fourth-grade school year. I left my home, family, job security, and support system to pursue my career and life goals. I brought as many of my belongings as possible with me on the plane and packed the rest in my car, which was shipped to me. I gave my furniture away to family members and sold a few pieces to my tenants. I started my new life in Maryland with an empty two-bedroom apartment and my only child.

Two months into my new job at the university I knew that it was not the place for me. I decided that this was going to be my last job but before I left, I would make a name for myself and build my network. I told myself that everyone would know my name. I ended up staying at that job for nearly four years. However, in another act of faith, I incorporated my consulting firm, Cause Engagement Associates (CEA) LLC in April 2015 while still employed at the university. CEA is the same company but with a different branding that I had attempted to launch in Las Vegas while working at the Health Department. In addition to branding, the only other difference between my new company and old one, New Era Public Health Group, is that CEA was successfully launched and has sustained with time. I will never forget the day that I snuck out and took an extra-long lunch break to drive to Baltimore to incorporate my business, which I operated for two years under the radar of my employer until the summer of 2017.

In July 2017, I was in my director's office with a colleague who was acting as my supervisor at the time. We were there for my performance review. During this time, I was eager to pursue my business full time, but I enjoyed some of the community engagement projects that I was working on for the center at the university. I told my director that I would eventually leave to pursue my consultancy business (that he did not know already existed) and would still like to work with him but in a different capacity as an independent contractor. He responded by saying, "if that time comes," and I interrupted him and said, "when that time comes," which prompted him to rephrase his sentence as follows "When that time comes, I will write you a letter of recommendation. I've brought you this far, haven't I?" Without hesitation, I responded by saying, "And I've brought you this far, haven't I? We have a mutually beneficial relationship." As soon as I walked out of that office, I knew that I could not work there much longer and needed to resign as soon as possible. October 31, 2017, was my last day. Since then, I have been one hundred percent self-employed.

It is often said that entrepreneurship is not for the faint of heart – i.e., those lacking the courage to face something difficult. While my journey continues and as rewarding as it is, I have and still face difficult times. As a single mother with no co-parenting support and lack of consistent and significant financial support outside of my own earnings, I have experienced periods of uncertainty that would break down someone without strong convictions and faith. There were times when I exhausted my business and personal bank accounts, maxed out credit cards, and received a personal loan from my bank to pay for my son's and my living expenses. However, through resilience and faith, I have never taken a side gig or part-time job to make extra income, even when I was broke and did not know where my next check was coming from.

In September 2018, I had $9 in my checking account! All I could do was get on the floor and cry. I said a prayer thanking God because I had faith that everything would be okay even though I did not know how. I did not know what to do next, but I knew that something would come my way as long as I did not give up. Luckily for me, I had a paid speaking engagement that week. I flew from the Baltimore-Washington area to Las Vegas on an all-expense paid trip to speak at a health care conference. I received a $500 check on the spot, which is a small change to some professional speakers, but it was a life saver for me at this time in my life.

This is where the miracle happens. During that same trip, I received an email notifying me that my company was awarded a $40k contract by the Maryland Department of Health. I forgot that I had submitted a proposal to the state to plan a series of violence prevention events. It was my first time submitting a proposal to the state, so I did not know what to expect. To this day, even though I experience occasional anxiety about income and business opportunities, I will not allow myself to worry about money or how I will make things happen for myself, my son, and my business. I dream, ask for guidance, do right by myself and others, and do my part by taking action and being ready to receive results. I have learned that every action taken by me yields rewards in some way in its own time. The key is to not give up on yourself, ask for guidance from God and the universe, and maintain some level of hope and faith. After all, as mentioned by Jesus' parable in Matthew 17:20, if you have faith that is the size of a grain of mustard seed, anything is possible.

My current leap of faith has led me to become an aspiring author, talk show host, and public figure who will continue to grow, learn, teach, and defy all limitations. I appreciate everyone who has joined me on this journey and allowed me to share myself with them through my various endeavors. In addition to helping people to help themselves and others, I hope that I can serve as a model for what others can achieve in all areas of their life even when I am facing challenging times, doubts, or confusion. "By faith he left Egypt, not fearing the king's anger; he persevered because he saw Him who is invisible," Hebrew 11:27.

# Your Thoughts
### *Perseverance, Resilience, and Faith*

What are your key takeaways from this chapter? On a scale from one to ten (ten being the highest), rate your level of perseverance, resilience, and faith. Do you give yourself enough credit? In which ways have you demonstrated these qualities? Be kind to yourself. Be proud of yourself.

# CHAPTER 7

## Life Visioning and Striving for Success

**In my journal entries** I shared my thoughts on the following themes: *Living Life in the Present Moment; Life Visioning; Striving for Success; and Life's Bucket List.* In this last chapter, I will share my current thoughts and progress in these different areas. First however I would like to highlight the fact that even though our lives can be broken down into different areas, it is important for us to acknowledge and understand that each area of our life is not independent of the other. For example, your physical health may impact your mental health, which in turn affects personal relationships and your job performance, which you rely on for financial stability. In my professional field of public health, we often refer to these areas as dimensions of wellness.

The most commonly referenced eight dimensions of wellness are the emotional, physical, occupational, intellectual, financial, social, environmental, and spiritual parts.[2] The idea or meaning of wellness refers to being healthy in many dimensions of our lives. However, given that we all have different experiences in life, wellness is more of a challenge for some people than others. With that said, my goal for myself and my wish for you are to reach and sustain full self-actualization, which is the realization or fulfillment of our talents and potential.

How do we reach the level of self-actualization? Well, according to psychologist Abraham Maslow (1908-1970), there is a hierarchy of human needs as displayed in the following pyramid. Needs lower down in the hierarchy at the bottom of the pyramid usually must be satisfied before individuals can attend to needs higher up in the hierarchy. The needs are physiological (food and clothing), safety (job security),

2   U.S. Department of Health and Human Services, Substance Abuse and Mental Health Services Administration. *Creating a Healthier Life: A Step-by-Step Guide to Wellness* (2016 SMA-16-4958). April 2016. Accessed October 23, 2021. https://store. samhsa.gov/product/Creating-a-Healthier-Life-/SMA16-4958.

love and belonging needs (friendship, love, and affection), esteem, and self-actualization.[3]

## Maslow Hierarchy of Needs[3]

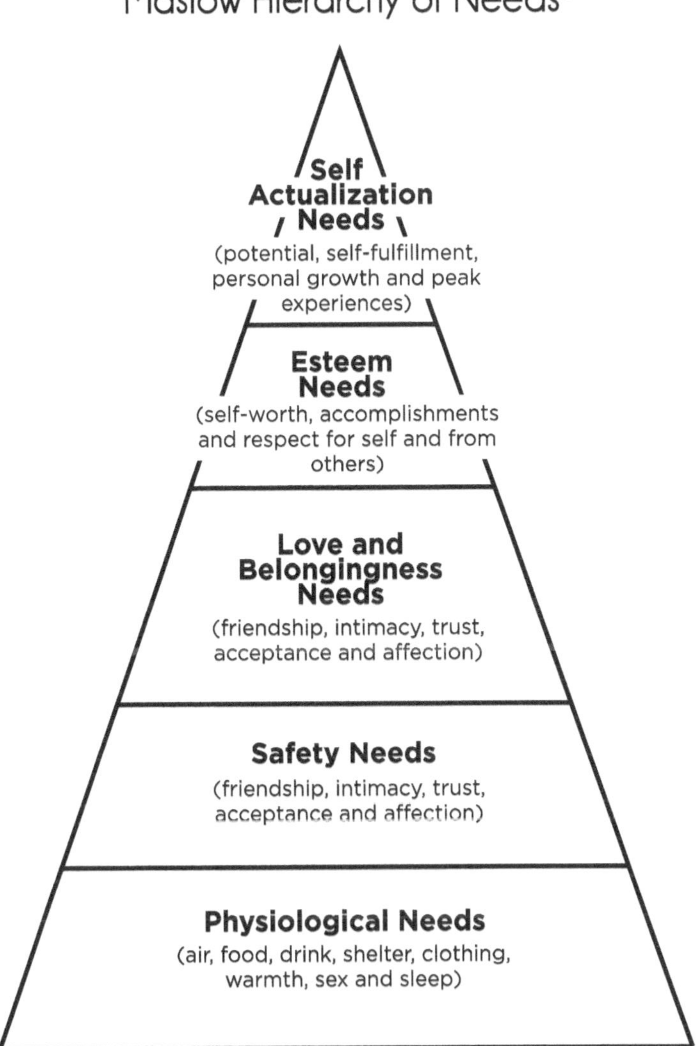



3   McLeod, Saul, A. "Maslow's hierarchy of needs." *Simply Psychology*. December 29, 2020. Accessed October 23, 2021. https://www.simplypsychology.org/maslow.html.

I personally do not want to spend my entire life just surviving and existing. As I revealed in previous chapters, I went through many phases of only having my basic needs met, but I always worked for more and consistently motivated and surrounded myself with people who in some form or the other contributed to or complimented my journey to success. I simply started with a dream or an idea, which brings us to the topic of life visioning.

As I expressed in *The Journal of a Woman with Lived Experiences*, life is about growth and change, and in my opinion, the best life lived is when you are intentional about that growth and change by creating a vision for life. Can your vision change? Yes. Will your vision change? Yes, most likely as you grow.

Creating a vision for yourself helps you to map out your path to achieving your life's goals. It helps you to determine what needs to be done and who you have to become to make your vision a reality. When times get tough, your vision should remind you of why you chose your path and what you are working towards. Your vision is also a way of manifesting what is to come but only if action, faith, and persistence are utilized.

As for living life in the present moment, that is really where I am at. While I have tangible goals for myself such as with cash, real estate, and a retirement portfolio, my overall vision for myself is to be happy, healthy, and to create memories for myself and with the people I love and care about such as my son, parents, family members, and close friends.

In my first book, I mentioned that I would definitely like a life partner, but I was not sure when or how that would happen. I still feel the same way because I know that I am on a journey, and where I am at today in life as it relates to my geographic location and life happenings is a part of the process. There are many doors for me to enter and places to go. I will meet him at the right time and when I do, we will continue on our life's journey together. I am not searching for love because that seems to be the one area in my life that I keep falling short in. However, this does not mean that I am not ready for love because I am, but I do understand that this is not something you can force on yourself or someone else. I believe in true love and will not settle for convenience.

I am not stuck in the past, and I am not so occupied with my future and the "what ifs" that I prevent myself from enjoying the fruits of life. In fact, I am very happy and proud of the life that I have created with God and His angels by my side. I want for nothing. Everything that I need is provided for me. I do not have the biggest or the most in my bank, but my lifestyle is what I always imagined for myself. I am available when my son needs me. I am not dependent upon another person or system to provide for me. When I am in need, I have my parents and family members that I can depend on. I am beautiful inside and out. I have no medical conditions, and the sky's the limit. Also, I am excited about helping my son to navigate through the next stage of his life – late adolescence – the transitional phase of growth and development between childhood and adulthood.

I still have my bucket list as well. Remember that I am not thinking about death, and you should not either. As I check things off my bucket list I will continue to add more. I do not worry about how I am going to accomplish the things on my list. It is really about enjoying life and having something to live for. Below is my update on the bucket list that I shared in my twenty-first journal entry in *The Journal of a Woman with Lived Experiences.*

**Things that remain on my bucket list:**

***Go-go dance for one night at a popular nightclub in a popular city.*** I have not checked this off of my bucket list and this is still something that I want to do. My first book was released shortly before the start of the COVID-19 pandemic and eventually everything was shut down. When I find a venue that I feel comfortable with I will definitely check off go-go dancing from my bucket list.

***Stand-up comedy for one night.*** Not yet. I cannot use COVID-19 as an excuse for this one. I just have to build up the nerve and start writing down my jokes that I often practice in the mirror. I am actually excited about it and will identify an amateur comedy spot to make my debut.

***Singing lessons.*** Nope, but a professional singer did tell me that I have a nice voice. Of the things left on my bucket list, this is not a top priority. However, I am starting to think that accomplishing the things on my bucket list is a good idea to carry out on a TV show.

***Preach a sermon.*** I am going to do this as a part of my book tour promotion. I am going to contact a church and ask if I can serve as a guest speaker. This will be my opportunity to deliver my message about faith and resilience in my own special way.

***Fall in love on a boat in the Mediterranean.*** About this, I am starting to waiver and will accept falling in love on a boat in the Caribbean. Nonetheless, I do believe that you can fall in love with the same person over and over again, and that is my plan. Any man who loves me will know that I am spoiled and hopefully will have no problem taking me to wherever I want to go, especially if it is going to cause me to fall more deeply in love with him.

***Visit Yellowstone Park and a summer road trip across the United States in a RV.*** This is something that was postponed because of the murder of Ahmaud Arbery by three white men in Georgia and protests across the United States after the murder of George Floyd by the Minnesota police officer, Derek Chauvin, as well as the political climate and the pandemic. I did not feel comfortable as a Black family traveling through predominantly white communities. However, I did move forward with my planning to visit Yellowstone Park and travel across the U.S. in a RV and will check these items off my bucket list soon.

***Tour museums and historic sites of Ethiopia.*** This dream was interrupted when the Ethiopian Prime Minister launched a civil war in the north of the country in November 2020. I pray for the souls of the victims of this war and for those who continue to suffer. My intent is to visit other countries in Africa.

***Travel the world collecting hand-made and custom jewelry.*** I started doing this during previous trips and will continue to do so. I intentionally seek to purchase from local women and to support fair and ethical trade.

**Things that I have checked off my bucket list:**

***Host my own TV show.*** Since I published my first book, I created two Internet talk shows on my YouTube channel, The Shawnta Jackson. I have conducted nearly eighty live interviews with individuals from all walks of life. My first show, "Live with Shawnta Jackson," featured discussions with individuals who had lived with experiences of trauma, triumph, healing, and motivation. One of my proudest moments and most memorable shows were my two interviews with Grammy Award Winner Anthony Hamilton. I also interviewed Dale Driscoll, a woman whose daughter, Helen, and twelve-year-old granddaughter, Brittany, were murdered in 2009 by Helen's ex-boyfriend. He had been released early from prison after serving only two and a half years of his sentence for assaulting his infant daughter which resulted in her having brain damage, but the record was not available for public viewing and Helen did not know. At the time of the interview, Dale, the mother and grandmother of the deceased, was working to pass legislation in New York State that would create a tracking system and public registry of domestic violence offenders. I interviewed so many great people with their own unique stories and am proud of my accomplishments.

I also hosted "Connections with Shawnta Jackson," a show I created to promote professional networking, career advancement, and business growth via unscripted live interviews with individuals who can inform and inspire. I interviewed community lawyers, public health professionals, and marketing consultants, but I think the highlights of this series were my interviews with John Brothers, President of the T. Rowe Price Foundation and President of T. Rowe Price Charitable and Franklyn Baker, President and CEO of United Way of Central

Maryland (UWCM). UWCM had recently received a $20 million donation from multi-billionaire philanthropist MacKenzie Scott. Again, I am proud of myself for having a vision and daring to execute it. In the upcoming years I plan to play around with different show concepts and look forward to sharing them with you.

***Write a book.*** Well, we know the answer to this. Not only did I write one book, but you are reading my second book now. I am very proud of myself for having the guts to share my most intimate and vulnerable thoughts with you. My intent is to help people by showing them that anything is possible, and to share my experiences and lessons learned as examples. Below is a review from a reader that exemplifies my intentions.

> *Shawnta Jackson is such a courageous woman. In The Journal of a Woman with Lived Experiences she shares her personal story of going from victim to victor. Then she peels back even more layers by sharing her personal journal entries, such as "my midsection is out of control." The journal entries are wrappers for profound life lessons. She invites us to journal our innermost private thoughts and embark on our own personal hero's journey. I loved when she wrote that "Giving up is easy. That's why most people do it." Thank God Shawnta didn't give up on herself and her mission. I loved this book and it's a great gift for everyone in your life who wants to experience phenomenal "Life Transformation."*
>
> *-LINDA HOLLANDER, CALIFORNIA*

When writing this book, I prayed before starting each chapter. I asked God to give me the right words to share. I was nervous about sharing my personal stories and even went through a phase of feeling unmotivated. I actually wanted not only to quit writing this book, but I wanted to quit all of my endeavors because I felt defeated. Yet, there is something in me that will not let me give up. I told myself that something great was coming my way and that it is the law of nature that where there is positive there is always negative, and that I could not let the negative overpower the positive and cause me to miss out on my blessings. My plan is to share this book with as many people as I can and to author additional books on various topics.

In closing, I hope by sharing the status of my bucket list that you are motivated to write down some things in life that you have always wanted to do. Create your own bucket list of things that you want to do in the near future and be brave enough to check them off and then add new things to your list. Wishing you love, peace, and blessings.

# *Your Thoughts*
## *Life Visioning and Striving for Success*

What are your key takeaways from this chapter? What is your vision for your life? What does success look like for you? Are you on the right path to achieving your goals? Why or why not? What are the five action steps that you can take within the next three to six months that will bring you closer to reaching or sustaining your life's vision and goals?

# DEAR READER,

**Thank you for taking** the time to read my second self-published book. I am curious to know what you think about this book, and how it has helped you. Please share your reviews. Also, be sure to tag me on Instagram and Facebook at @TheShawntaJackson and on Twitter @ShawntaTweets with your photos and videos. I will repost your testimonials and add them to my website at ShawntaJackson.com. If you would like to invite me to speak to your group or would like to interview me, please send an email to inquiries@shawntajackson.com.

Sincerely,

*Shawnta Jackson*

# ABOUT THE AUTHOR

Shawnta Jackson is that person who leaves a lasting impression. She motivates, challenges, and provides thought provoking solutions. She is a leader, mother, and social entrepreneur with a vision to help people help themselves and others.

In addition to writing, Shawnta helps organizations across the United States to plan, implement, and share the outcomes of their socially conscious initiatives. She also serves as a facilitator and guest speaker for various audiences.

She holds a Master of Public Health degree in social and behavioral health from University of Nevada, Las Vegas, and a Bachelor of Arts degree in public relations from Columbia College Chicago.

Shawnta resides in the Washington-Baltimore metropolitan area with her son, Zachary.

# REFERENCES

**Chapter 2: *The Benefits of Positive Affirmations and Gratitude***

1. Morin, Amy. "7 Scientifically Proven Benefits of Gratitude." *Psychology Today*. April 3, 2015. Accessed October 23, 2021. https://www.psychologytoday.com/us/blog/what-mentally-strong-people-dont-do/201504/7-scientifically-proven-benefits-gratitude.

**Chapter 7: *Life Visioning and Striving for Success***

2. U.S. Department of Health and Human Services, Substance Abuse and Mental Health Services Administration. *Creating a Healthier Life: A Step-by-Step Guide to Wellness* (2016 SMA-16-4958). April 2016. Accessed October 23, 2021. https://store.samhsa.gov/product/Creating-a-Healthier-Life-/SMA16-4958.

3. McLeod, Saul, A. "Maslow's hierarchy of needs." *Simply Psychology*. December 29, 2020. Accessed October 23, 2021. https://www.simplypsychology.org/maslow.html.